CR
6/13

D0576913

SUPER QUOTATION MARKS SAVES THE DAY!

SAN DIEGO PUBLIC LIBRARY
CHILDREN'S ROOM

3 1336 09236 1337

By Nadia Higgins • Illustrated by Mernie Gallagher-Cole

The Child's World®

Published by The Child's World®
1980 Lookout Drive • Mankato, MN 56003-1705
800-599-READ • www.childsworld.com

Acknowledgments
The Child's World®: Mary Berendes, Publishing Director
The Design Lab: Design and production
Red Line Editorial: Editorial direction

Design elements: Billyfoto/Dreamstime;
Dan Ionut Popescu/Dreamstime

Copyright © 2013 by The Child's World®
All rights reserved. No part of this book may be
reproduced or utilized in any form or by any means
without written permission from the publisher.

ISBN 9781614732723
LCCN 2012932877

Printed in the United States of America
Mankato, MN
July 2012
PA02117

About the Author: Nadia Higgins is a children's book author based in Minneapolis, Minnesota. Nadia has been a punctuation fan since the age of five, when she first wrote "Happy Birthday!" on a homemade card. "I love punctuation because it is both orderly and expressive," Nadia says. Her dream is to visit Punctuation Junction someday.

About the Illustrator: Mernie Gallagher-Cole is a freelance children's book illustrator living outside of Philadelphia. She has illustrated many children's books. Mernie enjoys punctuation marks so much that she uses a hyphen in her last name!

My name is Super Q. I am a pair of quotation marks. I show the exact words somebody said or wrote. Use me at the beginning and end of what was said.
I am Repeat. I say just what Super Q says. *Squaaaaawk!*

Sigh. Super Q stared at the ceiling. *SIGH.*
"Sigh," chirped Repeat, his parrot.

What a dull day to be a superhero in Punctuation Junction. Nobody had asked for help in days.

"I know," said Super Q, floating over to his computer. "I will offer my help."

Tap, tap, tap. Peck, peck, peck. He and Repeat worked on an ad for the daily newspaper.

Bang, bang, BANG! Just then, Ernest rushed into the room.
He was waving a sheet of paper. "Help!" he cried.

Looking at the paper, Super Q tried not to grin. This definitely looked like a job for a superhero.

"I had quotes in my story," Ernest explained. "Then, all at once, they just floated away. I called after them, but they did not even turn their heads. It was like they could not hear me. I tried to write without them. Now my story is a bore!"

"Hmmmmm," said Super Q.

"Hmmmmm," said Repeat.

"Someone has put the quotes under a spell," said Super Q. "And I know who it is." He pointed at a black smudge in the corner of Ernest's story. "This looks like the work of evil marker Mrs. Misquote."

"But what is she up to?" Ernest asked.

Super Q looked at the calendar. Repeat checked his watch. "Of course!" they both shouted.

"President Precise is giving a 'State of the Punctuation' speech today," Super Quote explained. "All the reporters are supposed to take notes on what she says for tomorrow's news. But if the quotes are under her evil spell . . ."

"Oh no!" cried Ernest.

"Hurry!" squawked Repeat.

And they all headed for town.

Punctuation, we should all be over the moon! Jobs for periods and commas are growing by leaps and bounds. Question marks are more questioning than ever. Quotation mistakes are at an end. . . .

When they arrived, the president was in full swing.

And there was not a moment to lose.
"Help, Super Q!" a reporter shouted.
"Our quotes are all wrong. The news is ruined!"

"Never fear!" cried Super Q.

And, with the power of *exact wording*, a dose of *true news*, and a bolt of *colorful stories*, Super Q broke the spell. He blasted Mrs. Misquote back to her dusty drawer.

"Our quotes are fixed," said the reporters. "You saved the news, Super Q!"

THE GREAT COOKIE CHEF

A short story by Ernest

Ken the question mark said,
"Cookies are so delicious! I love
to bake them." He told Kyra the
comma, "Oatmeal, sugar, and
chocolate-chip are the best to
make." "Could you bake me some
cookies, please?" Kyra asked Ken.
"Oh yes, Kyra," Ken exclaimed.
"I would love to bake you some
cookies!" Kyra was very happy!

The End

"And my story's gone from flat to fantastic," said Ernest.

"Fantastic," repeated Repeat.

Sigh. Super Q blushed with happiness.

PUNCTUATION FUN

Quotes can make a story come to life. Here is a story Pam the period wrote when the quotation marks were under Mrs. Misquote's evil spell. Now that the spell is gone, how could you use quotes to make this story better? Change this story to add three quotes. See how it comes to life.

Cory the comma had dreamed of this moment for years. He stared the Dark Wizard of Punctuation in the eye. The Dark Wizard told him all the evil, mean things he was going to do to Cory and his friends. Cory pretended he was not scared. He told the Dark Wizard to go away and leave them alone forever. The Dark Wizard said some more creepy things. So Cory cursed him with a magic spell. The spell had a lot of strange sounding words in it. The Dark Wizard screamed that he would come back and get them someday. Then he turned into a giant spider and crawled away.

DO NOT WRITE IN THE BOOK!

FUN FACTS

«You Can Quote Me»

In French, quotation marks look like a pair of sideways Vs. *«Bonjour!»* means "Hello!" in English.

Quote Inside a Quote

What if you are quoting somebody who is already quoting somebody else? So, for example, you are reporting about what Ernest shouted at Mrs. Misquote. This is how you would quote what Ernest said: "I cried out, 'You're doomed, Mrs. Misquote!'"

Let's take a closer look at that inside quote: 'You're doomed, Mrs. Misquote.' It's surrounded by a kind of punctuation called *single quotation marks*. They help the reader figure out who is talking when a story starts to get complicated.

Scare Quotes

Quotes around a word can also show that the word is not meant to be taken seriously. For example: Karen was "ready" for bed. (But all she had done was take off her shoes.) Quotes used this way are sometimes called scare quotes.

A Special Job

Quotes are also used around the titles of poems, songs, and other short works of art. For example: Ernest is the author of "The Great Cookie Chef."

Happy 400th Birthday!

How old is Super Q? Four hundred years, give or take. Use of quotation marks in written English dates back to the 1600s.